This book belongs to:

ATTICUS McGRAIN

2012 Xmas

Transport

ALAIN GRÉE

Transport

Button
BOOKS

First published 2012 by Button Books, an imprint of Guild of Master
Craftsman Publications Ltd, Castle Place, 166 High Street, Lewes,
East Sussex BN7 1XU.

Text © GMC Publications Ltd, 2012 Copyright in the Work © GMC
Publications Ltd, 2012 Illustrations © 2012 A.G. & RicoBel.

ISBN 978 1 90898 504 0
A catalogue record for this book is available from the British Library.

Publisher: Jonathan Bailey; Production Manager: Jim Bulley; Managing
Editor: Gerrie Purcell; Senior Project Editor: Dominique Page; Editor:
Virginia Brehaut; Managing Art Editor: Gilda Pacitti; Colour origination by
GMC Reprographics; Printed and bound in China by Leo Paper Products.

On the road

caravan

taxi

bus

Lots of different vehicles use the road every day, making it a busy place. How many of these have you seen?

motorbike

bicycle

delivery van

car

moped

7

Types of car

Cars are made in many different shapes, sizes and colours. Can you see one that you have travelled in?

early motor car

small family car

open-topped sports car

racing car

four-wheel-drive car

What's inside a car?

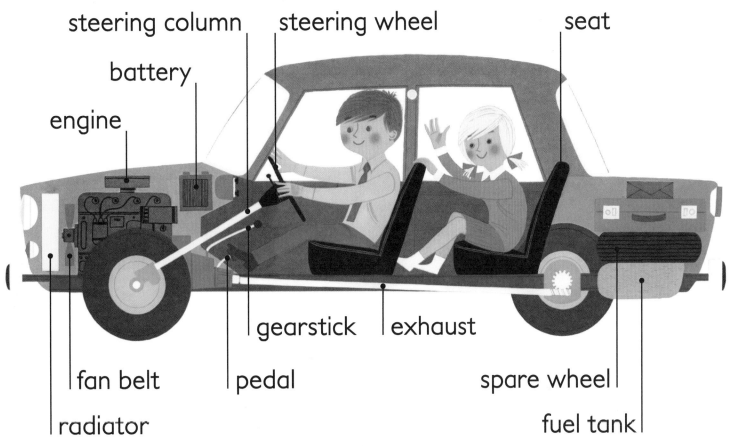

steering column   steering wheel   seat

battery

engine

fan belt   pedal

radiator

gearstick   exhaust

spare wheel

fuel tank

How a car is made

The frame, doors and body are put together...

Next, the dashboard, headlamps,

...engine, wheels, windows, bumpers and seats are fitted.

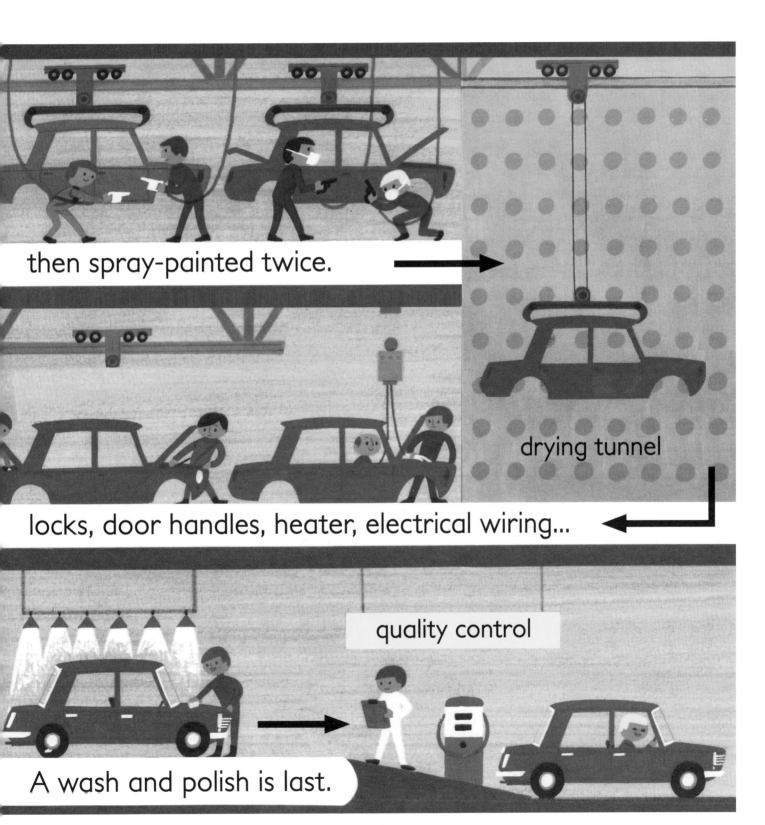

then spray-painted twice.

drying tunnel

locks, door handles, heater, electrical wiring...

quality control

A wash and polish is last.

At the garage

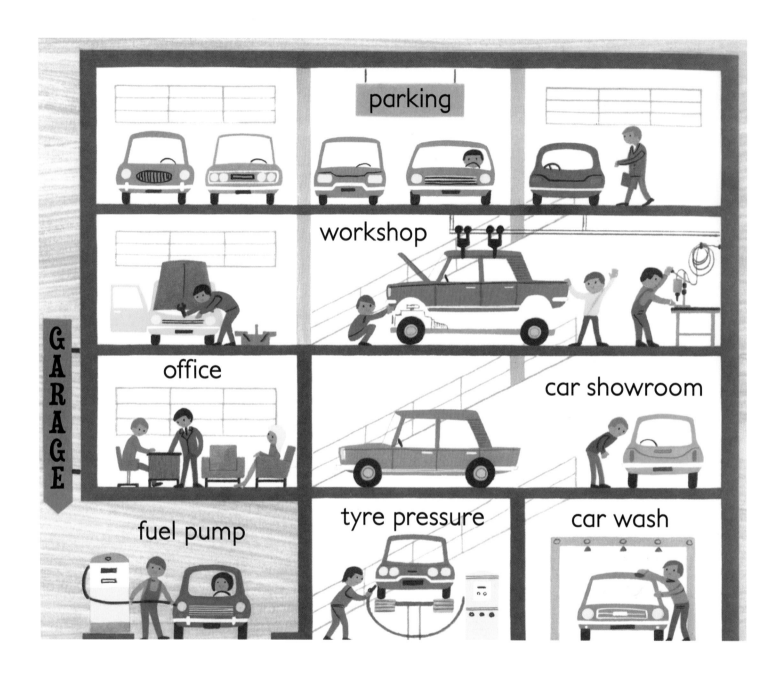

This garage is a very busy place. We go there to buy fuel or have our car fixed by a mechanic.

Most vehicles need fuel to run on. This is delivered to the garage in a large tanker.

fuel tanker

fuel can and oil

fuel pump

Trucks and lorries

These large vehicles can transport very bulky materials or tow a trailer. We like to watch them at work. Which do you think carries the heaviest load?

pick-up truck

lorry

dumper truck

Emergency vehicles

These vehicles will come to
help in an emergency and
keep everybody safe.

fire engine

ambulance

police car

Two-wheeled vehicles

moped

motorbike

delivery bicycle and trailer

Railways

Trains run on railway tracks that link cities, towns and villages together. Sometimes there are tunnels to go through or special crossings for cars and trains.

level crossing

Types of train

steam train

The first trains were pulled by steam engines. Today, most trains are powered either by electricity or diesel.

passenger train

electric train

diesel freight train

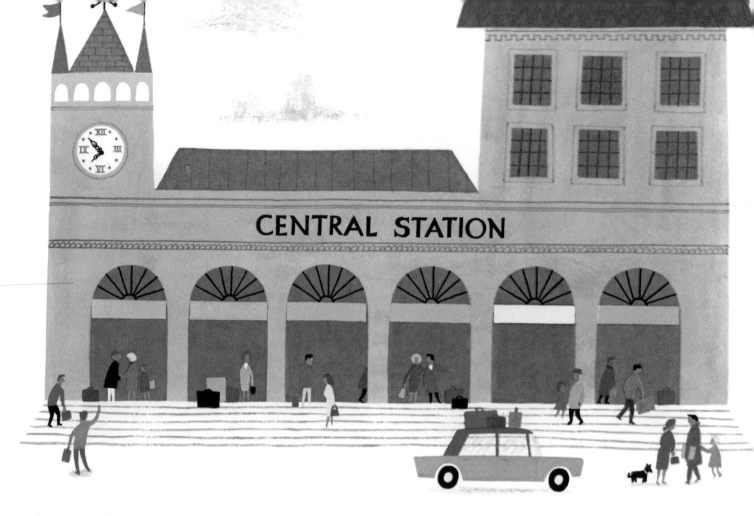

At the railway station

The railway station is very crowded with passengers arriving and departing.

20

clock

passengers

luggage trolley

station master

'What time will our train leave?' we ask the station master. 'At quarter past four', he says. 'Platform one – better hurry!'

21

Railway signals

Trains must follow signals at a junction,
just like cars follow traffic lights on the road.
The passengers wait patiently for the train
to continue its journey.

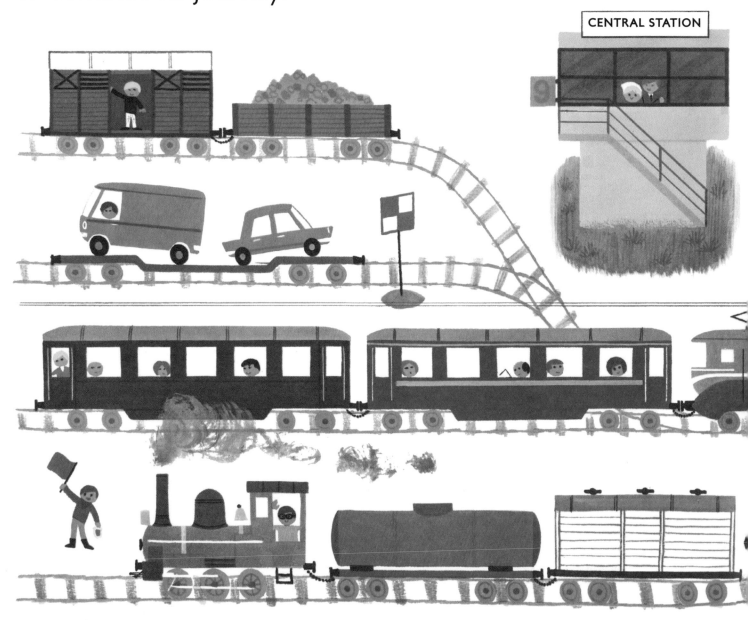

CENTRAL STATION

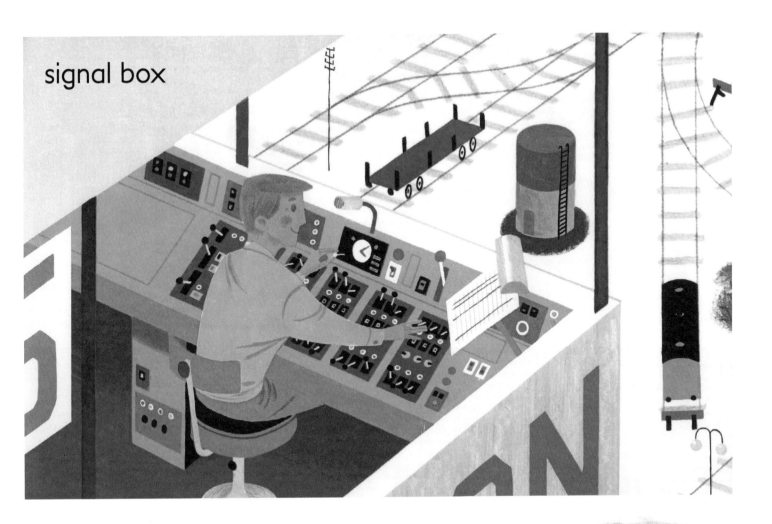

signal box

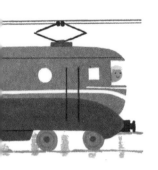

The signal operator has
a very important job,
making sure that each
train is on the right track.

signal

Underground trains

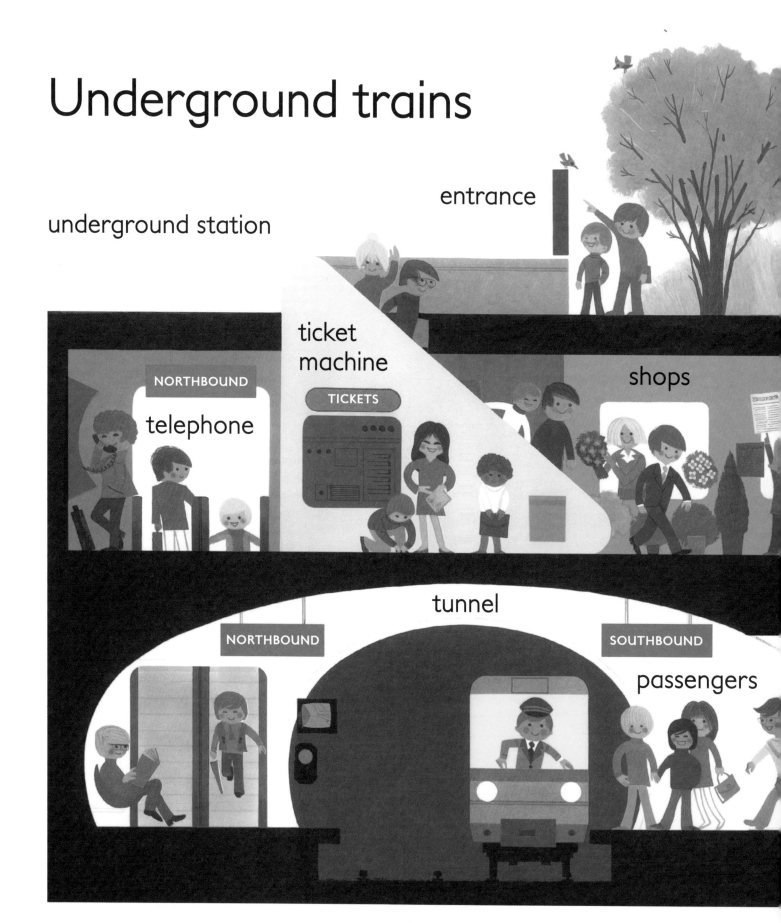

underground station

entrance

ticket machine

TICKETS

shops

NORTHBOUND

telephone

tunnel

NORTHBOUND

SOUTHBOUND

passengers

SOUTHBOUND

escalator

Travelling beneath the streets by underground train is a quick way to get around the city.

The trains travel fast through underground tunnels, leaving the streets above clear for road traffic.

underground trains

WAY OUT

CIRCLE

On the water

We can travel in boats on the sea, rivers or canals.
The children enjoy watching the boats go underneath
the bridge and wonder where they are going.

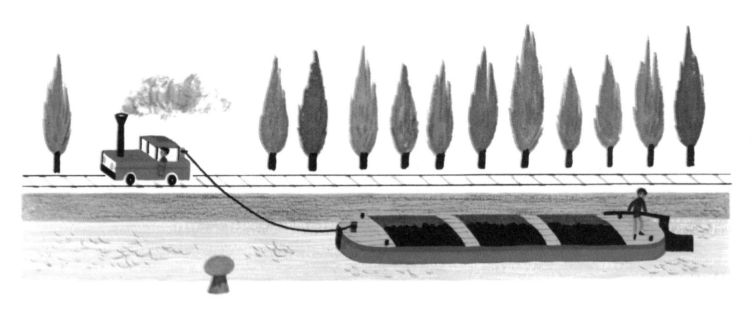

Sometimes boats carry cargo instead of passengers.

What are they loading onto this cargo boat?

27

Types of boat

The first boats were simply logs tied together to make a floating raft. Today, huge ships can carry passengers, cargo and even lorries.

raft

Viking longboat

Native American canoe

pirate's ship

sailing boat

dinghy

steam riverboat

ocean liner

speedboat

29

An ocean liner

The largest ocean liners are like floating towns, with bedrooms, shops, restaurants and even cinemas on board. When an ocean liner arrives at its destination a small boat, called a tug, is used to guide it into the port.

Inside a liner

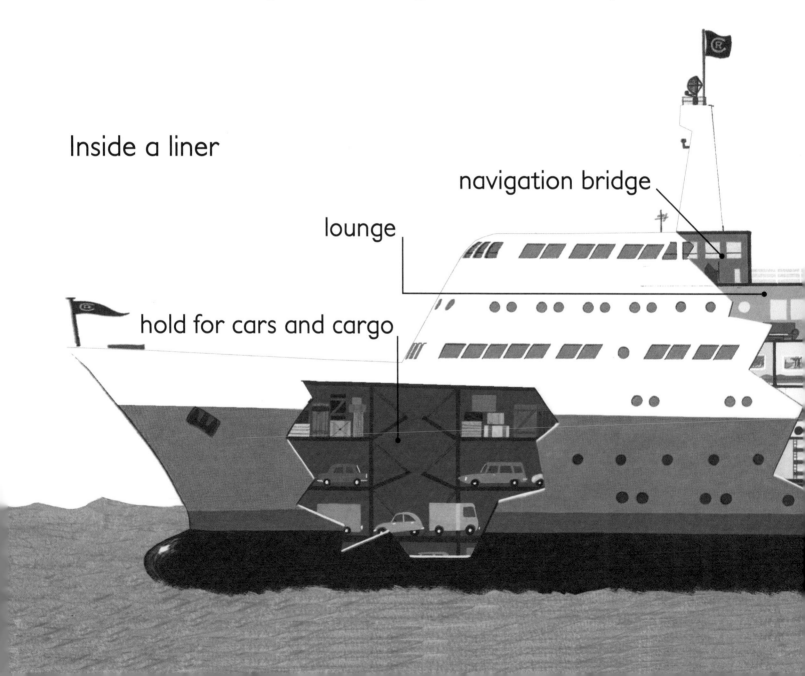

navigation bridge

lounge

hold for cars and cargo

tug

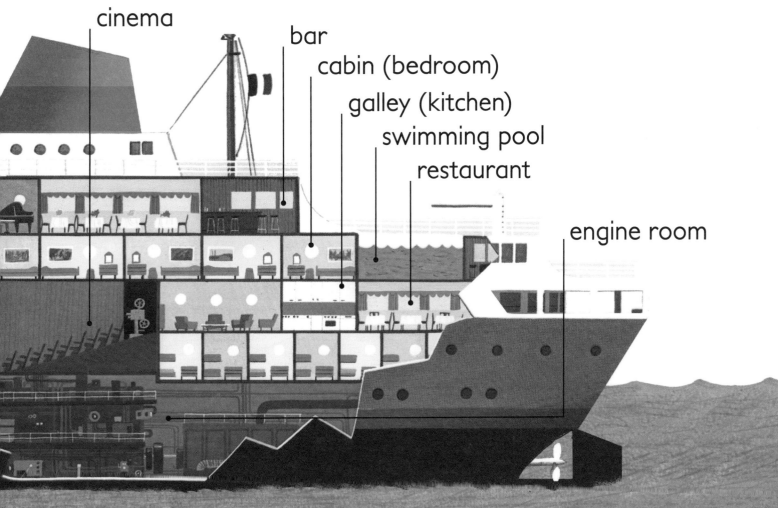

cinema

bar

cabin (bedroom)

galley (kitchen)

swimming pool

restaurant

engine room

On a boating holiday

Boats can be used for having fun with family and friends. We like to relax on the boat, but children must play carefully near the water.

On a boating holiday we can go swimming, fishing, snorkelling and bird watching. We like to play out in the fresh air with our friends. What else is fun to do on a boat?

What's inside a motor boat?

crew's cabin (bedroom)

fuel tank

engine

controls

galley (kitchen)

A modern motor boat has
everything you need on holiday.
There are even beds and a kitchen.

dining cabin

portholes

storage

bed

anchor

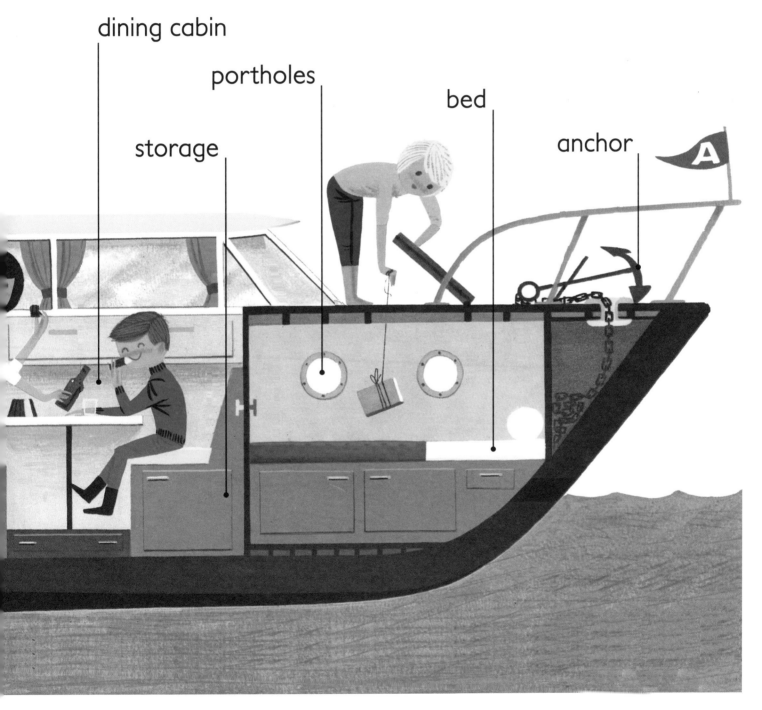

Up in the air

We can travel through the air to go on a journey, or sometimes just for fun. Everything looks very small from up high in the sky. What can you see from up here?

parachutes

Whee! It is great fun
to be up in the air!

hot-air balloon

helicopter

M-1751

29

Types of aeroplane

Modern planes have a jet
engine or use propellers to
fly. Gliders use the currents
in the air to transport them.

early aeroplane

propeller plane

seaplane

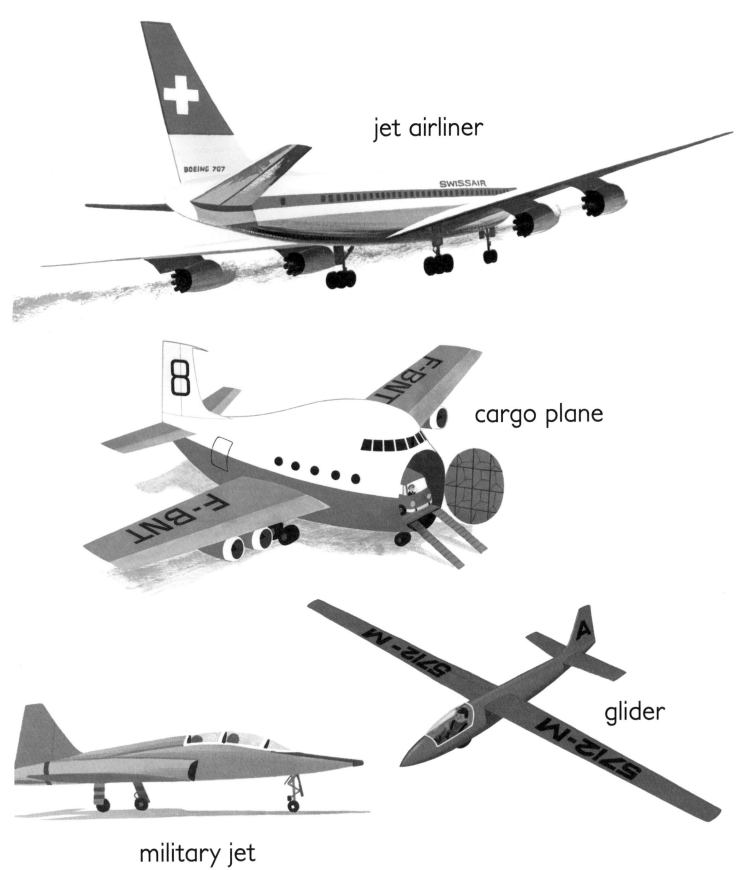

jet airliner

cargo plane

glider

military jet

At the airport

Planes take off from and land at the airport, bringing passengers and their luggage from far away.

Between trips, the planes are refuelled, cleaned and made ready for their next flight.

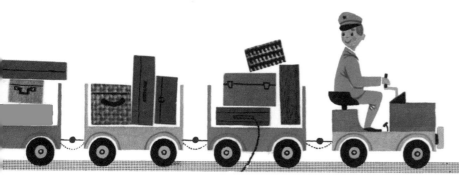

luggage cart

aeroplane

40

fuel truck

water

passenger bus

What's inside an aeroplane?

The passengers sit in long, narrow rows while the flight attendants look after them. The pilot sits at the front to fly the plane and perform take-off and landing.

Inside a jet airliner

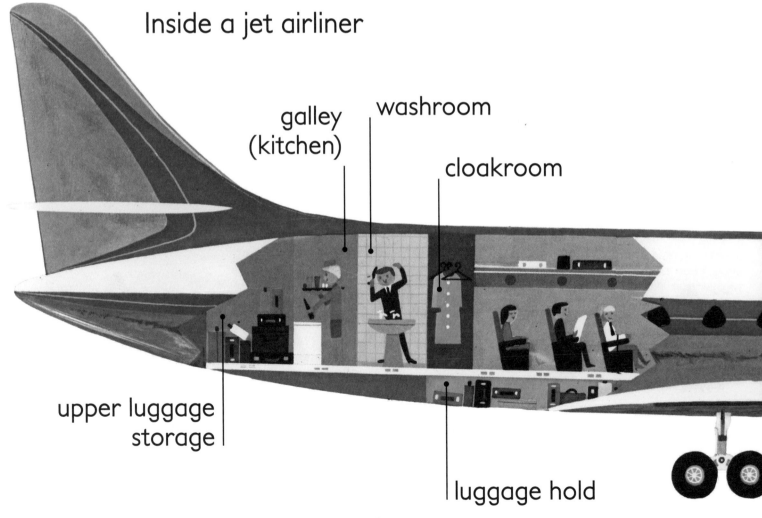

galley
(kitchen)

washroom

cloakroom

upper luggage
storage

luggage hold

Inside a jet plane

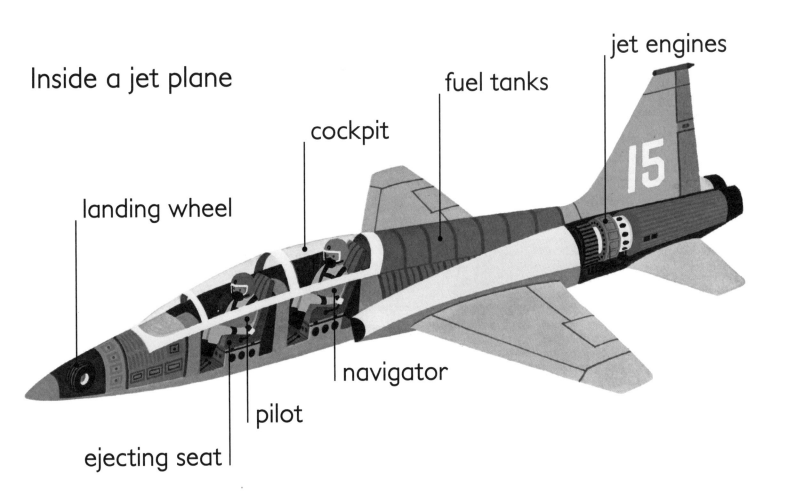

jet engines

fuel tanks

cockpit

landing wheel

15

navigator

pilot

ejecting seat

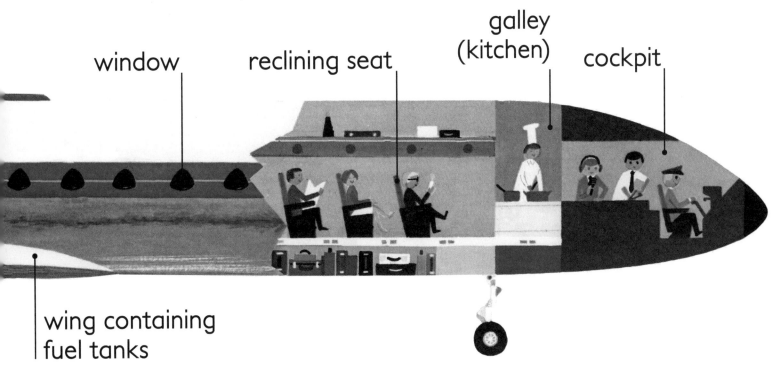

window

reclining seat

galley
(kitchen)

cockpit

wing containing
fuel tanks

Uncle Jim is a pilot. He has been on a trip to France and brought us back a present. Can you guess what it is?

44

Hooray, it is a model aeroplane!
Thank you very much, Uncle Jim.

Travelling into space

A space rocket can fly even higher than an aeroplane to explore outer space. Its crew are called astronauts.

Astronauts can travel on the surface of the moon in a moon buggy designed for these special conditions.

astronauts

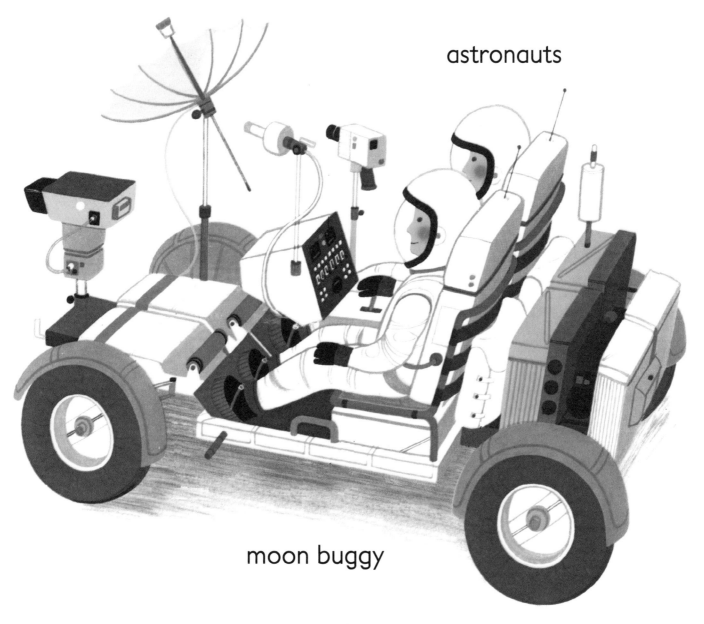

moon buggy

ALAIN GRÉE

For more on Button Books, contact:

GMC Publications Ltd
Castle Place, 166 High Street, Lewes, East Sussex, BN7 1XU
United Kingdom
Tel +44 (0)1273 488005
www.gmcbooks.com